Fabric +
Paint +
Thread =
Fabulous

Pat Durbin

Martingale®
& COMPANY

Fabric + Paint + Thread = Fabulous
© 2009 by Pat Durbin

That Patchwork Place® is an imprint of
Martingale & Company®.

Martingale & Company
20205 144th Ave. NE
Woodinville, WA 98072-8478 USA
www.martingale-pub.com

Credits

President & CEO: Tom Wierzbicki

Editor in Chief: Mary V. Green

Managing Editor: Tina Cook

Developmental Editor: Karen Costello Soltys

Technical Editor: Ellen Pahl

Copy Editor: Melissa Bryan

Design Director: Stan Green

Production Manager: Regina Girard

Illustrator: Laurel Strand

Cover & Text Designer: Stan Green

Photographer: Brent Kane

Photo Stylist: Peg Kane

Printed in China
14 13 12 11 10 09   8 7 6 5 4 3 2 1

**Library of Congress Cataloging-in-Publication Data
is available upon request.**

ISBN: 978-1-56477-937-3

Mission Statement

Dedicated to providing quality products and service to inspire creativity.

Dedication

To my family—I am blessed by each of you.

Acknowledgments

I am grateful for my heritage. Strong people of faith and character are scattered through the family tree. I look back also to a wealth of women who held a needle not only out of necessity, but also from a love of the art. I learned early to appreciate the art of sewing. It has always been a part of who I am.

I am most thankful for my husband, Gary. What a wonderful man. We've lived through a lot of things together, some very good, some very challenging. His love and support have kept me going—most of the time with a smile. His help in my quilting adventure is immeasurable. To mention just a few things, he's my photographer, adviser, handyman, exhibit hanger, proofreader, and my greatest fan.

Thanks also to my quilting friends. I won't name all of you, but you know you've played a role in my success. As artists of any kind, we must encourage and cheer our peers. That encouragement greases the wheels of inspiration and creativity.

Thanks to the staff at Martingale & Company for the many ways in which you make the finished book come together.

Treasures: *Grandmother Jennie Bunch Haines and her Wedding Ring quilt; my mother, Sanna Haines Heberly, and her crocheted chair decoration, draping gracefully over the side of Great-Grandmother Bunch's sewing basket; Great-Aunt Ruth Heberly Selves and her Butterfly quilt; and Grandfather Homer Haines's Bible*

Contents

Introduction
and Inspiration » 6

The ABCs of Fabulous
Picture Quilts » 7

Quiltmaking Basics » 58

About the Author » 63

Resources » 63

Floral Palette » 30

PROJECTS

Island Sunrise » 14

Wonderland » 40

Lacy Leaves Table Runner
and Napkins » 22

Lakeside » 50

Introduction and Inspiration

AAH . . . FABRIC, THREAD, BEAUTIFUL COLORS, AND PATTERNS! THE QUILT IS MY WAY TO EXPRESS THE JOY I FEEL OBSERVING CREATION. AND I USE MIXED MEDIA—FABRIC, PAINT, AND THREAD—TO CREATE MY ART AND INFUSE IT WITH TEXTURE AND DEPTH.

In my quilting life, I have become consumed with pictorial quilts. I am inspired by the beautiful images of the creation around me—light on the bay, dew on the grass, a baby laughing, to name a few. Landscapes, people, and animals all get into my brain. My goal is to make quilts that look as much like those images as I can. Sometimes it can be difficult to duplicate an idea in fabric; I have been experimenting and discovering new ways to get the effect I want.

My goal in this book is to pass on a few tidbits I've learned to help you have fun with new techniques or ways of doing things that you've perhaps not tried before. For example, trees are very inspiring to me. I have experimented with what I call "thread motifs" to make trees look more leafy and realistic. I now use this method for other design elements as well, and I will be sharing this technique with you.

I have always wanted to paint. However, I never really experimented with painting until a few years ago when I needed help achieving a certain effect on one of my quilts. Now I really appreciate what paint on fabric can do.

When making the projects for this book, I've tried to suggest a variety of ways to use the techniques. Maybe you'll look at one and say, "Hey, that might work on that special quilt I've wanted to make." I would be very pleased by that.

You certainly don't have to be an expert quiltmaker to try any of the techniques in this book. Just jump in and give it a whirl! I think you'll be surprised by how much fun it is.

The ABCs of Fabulous Picture Quilts

BEFORE YOU BEGIN, BE SURE TO READ THROUGH THIS SECTION FOR USEFUL INFORMATION ABOUT SUPPLIES, PAINTING ON FABRIC, AND PLAYING WITH THREAD TECHNIQUES. YOU WILL BE REFERRED BACK TO THESE TIPS WHEN MAKING THE PROJECTS.

Basic Supplies

You'll need the basic sewing supplies listed below. Specific products and tools for painting and thread play are discussed later.

- Rotary cutter
- Rotary-cutting mat, 18" x 24"
- Acrylic ruler, 6" x 24", for rotary cutting
- Square ruler, 12½" x 12½" (optional, but helpful for squaring up the quilt)
- Scissors for cutting fabric
- Scissors for cutting paper
- Sewing machine with a walking foot and free-motion foot
- Straight pins
- Safety pins
- Machine needles for piecing and quilting
- Paper-backed fusible web
- Spray sizing

Fabrics

Fabrics for painting should be solid white or slightly off-white 100% cotton. Buy good-quality fabric with a high thread count. It will give you a much smoother surface than inexpensive muslin. Always prepare the fabric by washing it to remove sizing, but don't use any fabric softeners, because they may inhibit the paint from sticking.

Fabrics for piecing, borders, backing, and binding can be beautiful prints or batiks, but they should all be 100% cotton.

Supplies needed for thread play and painting on fabric

Let's Paint

Painting on fabric is a completely different world from painting on paper or canvas. Here are some important things to remember:

- Fabric acts as a wick! You will find that your paint will walk along the weave of the fabric (sometimes farther than you had planned).

- Wet fabric will wick the paint faster, and the colors will blend together easily. You can use this to your advantage to blend colors.

- The first coat of paint will soak into the fibers and spread easily. It will also fill up the spaces and change the texture of the fabric. Fabric on which paint has already dried will accept additional paint in a completely different way. The second coat will lie *on top of* the paint, rather than soaking into the fabric as the first coat did. If the first layer isn't too dark, you can usually paint over it with another color.

Fabric Paints

My first choice for painting on fabric is SoSoft acrylic paint by DecoArt, because it does not need to be heat-set, and it remains soft to the touch after drying. I have used this product line for the examples in this book, and the materials section for each project lists the specific colors I chose. SoSoft works well for controlled painting when you want to create images with hard lines, and it also blends nicely with water to create skies or waterscapes. Of course, you may substitute similar colors of other brands if you choose. There are several other brands on the market that are very nice paints, but please test them first as described in "Test Run" on page 10. Also check to see if they need to be heat-set, and follow the manufacturer's instructions for usage.

Water Barriers

You will need a waterproof material underneath your fabric when painting, to protect the work surface.

Foam core board. This product is very handy if you plan to do more than a few projects. I suggest purchasing a 20" x 30" or 30" x 40" piece, available at art supply and craft stores. I cover it with clear or white contact paper, which wipes clean easily. This gives you a nice smooth surface to paint on.

Clear cellophane. Cellophane makes a good barrier, but you must be careful not to tear it. It comes on rolls in the wrapping paper section of craft stores. I often transfer the outline of the design directly onto the cellophane with a Sharpie permanent pen, allowing me to use the cellophane as a guide for painting as well as a water barrier. The lines will show through the white fabric.

Freezer paper. Used shiny side up, freezer paper is another option for small projects. You can also transfer a design onto it to serve as a guide when painting.

Vinyl. A sheet of lightweight vinyl is useful for covering your table, easel, or ironing board. I often use it on the floor or on the table in addition to another water barrier to protect the surface from stray drops of paint. Look for this in fabric stores that carry vinyl for tablecloths.

Other Painting Supplies

The items listed here will help you efficiently carry out, and clean up after, your painting adventures.

Paint palette. A palette can be purchased for very little in a craft store, or a plastic lid from a whipped topping container works fine too.

Water container. Keep a container of water close by to rinse your brushes.

Spray mist bottle. Fill a spray bottle with clean water and use this to dampen the fabric.

Paintbrushes. Buy brushes of good quality that will last. My favorite brush is a flat shape with a tapered tip. I can get a broad stroke or a fine line with it, and can even use the point for dots. I have several other brushes in various shapes—both round and fine-line. As you work, you will develop a preference for the type you like best.

Natural sponges. A natural sponge is one that grew in the ocean; it is not synthetic. It has large, uneven openings and cleans up easily. I use these sponges for applying paint to large areas and especially for wet-on-wet painting. They are great when I want to create skies and blend colors. Because of the uneven texture, I also use a natural sponge and the dry-on-dry paint technique for shrubs and tree shapes.

Paper towels. Keep paper towels and a trash can handy for cleanup. You can also mop up with scrap fabric or rags, if you prefer.

Wet-on-Wet Painting

I like this method for sky or water backgrounds. If you want colors to blend smoothly from one to the next, spray your fabric with a mist of water, and dilute your paints by adding water. Then apply colors to the fabric and let them bleed from one to the other. Keep the fabric lying flat if you want the colors to stay where you put them.

> **QUICK STOP FOR PAINT**
> If your paint is moving faster than you want it to, try using a hair dryer on a low setting to speed up the drying process.

Dry-on-Dry Painting

There are times when you'll want a hard line between colors, such as a horizon line or an outline of a defined shape. To achieve a crisp line, you'll have to trick the fabric into submission and use the dry-on-dry method. Use dry fabric, a dry brush, and undiluted paint. You can paint up to, or on top of, an already painted area (that has been allowed to dry) with good results. Before using this method, always do a test on a scrap of the same fabric that you plan to use in your final piece, so you will know if it works in an acceptable way.

Don't leave any pools or drops of excess paint, because any paint will wick into the fabric if there is too much left on the surface. Let one application of paint dry completely before you paint up to it with an additional color. The dry paint will act as a barrier between the sections. Be careful, however, not to let misted water or the newly applied wet paint seep under the line. Use a hair dryer if this starts to happen.

TEST RUN

Always test the fabric and paint that you plan to use.

Wet test. Use two different paint colors and a wet brush. Slightly dampen the fabric with clean water from a spray bottle. Squeeze a small amount (about ⅛ teaspoon) of each color onto your palette and dilute it with a drop of water. Paint a dab of one color, and then near to it paint a dab of another color. Watch what happens. Do they travel and seep into each other? That's what I want to see for the wet-on-wet technique.

Dry test. Use a flat or tapered dry brush on dry fabric. Paint a narrow line, straight or curvy, using paint directly from the jar with no water added. If your paint stays where it is supposed to and dries without traveling away from the line, you have a paint-and-fabric combination that will be acceptable to work with.

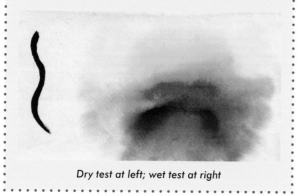

Dry test at left; wet test at right

Helpful Tips

■ Always cut your background fabric at least 1" larger than the desired finished size to allow a margin for trimming later.

■ When painting a picture with many different elements, paint one section at a time and let it dry completely before moving to the next section. If you have layered images such as a tree over a sky background, paint the tree last, dry on dry, over the background paint.

■ Use paintbrushes and natural sponges for different textures. My favorite brush is a flat, tapered brush, but I probably use my sponge even more often than a brush.

■ As you work on your composition, be sure to step back and observe it from a distance frequently. Don't be afraid to add some colors that I haven't listed if you see a need for them. It's your picture; my directions are there only to guide you in your own artistic adventure.

■ If you don't have all the paint colors that you need, remember the color wheel. You can blend any color using the three primary colors: yellow, red, and blue. You can make pastels by adding white or adding water; make shades by adding black. It's a little more work, and you might have trouble duplicating the color if you run out, but this can be fun. It's kind of like coloring with a box of 8 crayons instead of a box of 120!

■ Place a pressing cloth on your ironing board, and then press the finished painting on the wrong side with a warm iron after it has dried completely.

Let's Play with Thread

I like to use beautiful threads to enhance my picture quilts. I use them in two ways—in machine quilting, and in creating thread motifs to apply to my projects. I create thread motifs such as lacy leaves, palm trees, or evergreen treetops separately at my sewing machine, and then add them to the quilt top. When the quilt is complete, I machine quilt it using additional decorative threads and stitch designs that will enhance the painted images. (Note that these painted quilts are not good candidates for hand quilting.)

Fall leaves

Foundations and Tools

Tulle. The same fabric that is used for bridal veils makes a wonderful foundation for the threadwork in these projects. Tulle is very fine nylon netting, and it is available at fabric stores in many colors. Sometimes you will find it shiny, or embellished with glitter. It's fun stuff.

Water-soluble stabilizer. Used with the tulle, stabilizer creates a base on which to stitch your thread motifs. Use a water-soluble stabilizer such as Solvy or Dissolve that dissolves completely in water after the stitching is done.

Embroidery hoop. A hoop will hold the motif taut to keep it from drawing up tight with all the thread as you stitch. Make sure you use a hoop that lies very flat, and choose one that is 5" or 7" in diameter with a pinch-release mechanism. The pinch release allows you to easily reposition the hoop as needed when stitching. To move it, stop sewing, leave the needle down, release the hoop, scoot the bottom ring to where you want it, and reattach the top ring. You can hold onto the pincher and the edge of the hoop with your fingers to maneuver it around while stitching.

Threads

Choices, choices! We have a multitude of choices for thread. Let's take advantage of them to create even more beautiful art quilts.

Threads are an important part of this book. The top thread feeds from the spool and passes through the needle; the bobbin thread is wound onto the bobbin. I like the thread on top to shine and often use rayon or other threads with sheen for this. You may use whatever threads you like, but I will share my preferences. I do not recommend metallic threads, because they tend to break easily.

Look outside at a leafy tree. See how there are dark shadows, and bright, light areas—sometimes almost white—where the sun hits it. A variety of thread colors will help you achieve more realistic artistry. You'll need lights, darks, true colors, and dull colors to make your pictures come alive. I like to use a lot of variegated threads. Stock up on threads when they go on sale at your local fabric store.

Top thread. You have many beautiful choices when it comes to the thread you use on the top of your quilt. The company Superior Threads offers some great products: I like Trilobal polyester, which comes in many colors, both solid and variegated, and I use their MonoPoly (invisible) for attaching finished thread motifs to the quilt. Sulky Threads produces rayon thread that comes in many colors—solids and variegated—and creates a nice sheen on the quilt. Signature and YLI are two more resources for beautiful threads. I know there are many more, but these are the ones that I find where I shop. Check out your own local quilt shop for a variety, and look for pretty colors that will blend to make your artwork special.

Bobbin thread. For building thread motifs, use a cotton or cotton blend on the bobbin. A 40-weight thread will help to build up the thread quickly. The bobbin thread will show through the tulle somewhat; if you use one color in the bobbin and another on top, you will get double duty out of the sewing you do and your trees will look more realistic. For heavy machine quilting and free-motion quilting, I like to use Bottom Line by Superior Threads for the bobbin. This fine, 60-weight thread allows the top threads to do their best without creating a thick buildup of threads on the bottom.

Setting Up the Sewing Machine for Thread Play

Your individual machine is going to dictate the setup. You need a darning foot or free-motion quilting foot for thread play. Drop the feed dogs on your machine or cover them with a card that has a hole punched in the middle for the needle to go through.

Tension. Make sure your tension is correct. The goal is to have the bobbin thread lie nicely on the bottom of the piece without popping its head up on top; the top thread should look even on top and not do any loopy things on the back. Keep scrap fabric at hand to test threads and tension often, so you don't have nasty surprises to pick out. Some decorative threads will require loosening the top tension a bit. Lower numbers equal looser tension.

Needle. I use an 80/12 topstitch needle. The larger hole in this needle allows room for the fancier threads to fly through without shredding.

Stitch. Zigzag stitches of varying widths are most often my choice for the motifs, although I have used straight stitching at times.

Thread. I use 40-weight threads in both the bobbin and on top. I use cotton or a blend in the bobbin. On top I use threads of Trilobal polyester or rayon because I like the sheen. Cotton also works fine if you prefer it. Refer to "Top Thread" and "Bobbin Thread" on page 11 for additional details.

DOUBLE THE FUN

Using two threads on top is an interesting option for thread play. My machine has two thread holders, so I can thread one below the tension disk and one on top of the tension disk. Both threads go through the same eye (hole) in the needle. I can use one color for the bobbin and two different colors on top, creating a nice blend with just one sweep of the needle. If your machine doesn't have two spool holders, it may be possible to use a straw to extend the upright spool holder so that it will accommodate two spools, one on top of the other. This might take a bit of experimentation. Don't fight your machine if it doesn't want to do this; the thread-play method works fine with only one top thread.

Stitching the Thread Motifs

1. Transfer the outline of the design to water-soluble stabilizer with a permanent pen.

2. Place a layer of tulle on top of the stabilizer and pin the corners temporarily. The tulle will become a permanent part of the motif.

3. Secure the two layers in a pinch-release flat embroidery hoop.

Design ready to stitch

4. Begin by taking one stitch, and then pull the bobbin thread to the top. Hold both threads as you begin stitching until you're about ¼" to ½" away. Stop and clip the thread tails close to the surface. Use a zigzag stitch to fill in the design, or stitch as instructed in each of the projects.

5. To end your stitching, take several stitches in one place to lock the thread. Raise the foot and move the motif away from the needle; clip the top and bottom threads close to the surface. Change threads often to add interest.

6. When you are satisfied, audition the thread piece on your quilt to see if you want to add any additional thread or thread colors.

Finishing the Thread Motifs

1. Once you have completed stitching the thread motif, soak the piece in cool water for about 15 minutes to remove the stabilizer. Drain the water and repeat. Check by touch and sight to see if the stabilizer is gone, and then rinse one final time.

2. Roll the thread motif in a terry towel and squeeze out most of the water. Lay the piece on an ironing board, stretching it out a little and pinning to hold it in place. Allow to air-dry. **Caution:** Do not use a hot iron on tulle. The heat will destroy the tulle and many synthetic threads.

3. Use small, blunt-tipped scissors to carefully trim around the thread motif. Remove as much tulle as practical, trying not to cut any of the thread. Hold the motif over a piece of white paper as you trim so that you can see the tulle more clearly. The paper will also catch the tiny pieces you cut away.

4. Stitch the motif to the quilt top with monofilament thread on top.

Thread Painting While Quilting

Thread painting is really just heavy machine quilting done in an artistic way. As I do this type of quilting, I feel like I'm still painting and adding details to the picture.

You'll need to be friendly with your sewing machine, because these quilts need to be machine quilted. Students often ask, "Do I really need a free-motion or darning foot to do thread painting?" My answer is, "Yes, you really do!"

I often use a zigzag stitch to add texture to leafy spots, and I change thread colors frequently. Use a 60-weight polyester bobbin thread in the bobbin, and a 40-weight thread in the needle. With a very lightweight thread in the bobbin, you can stitch more thread on the surface of the quilt without drawing up the layers too much. Check the thread tension before beginning. You may need to loosen it on top.

Be sure to add a consistent amount of quilting over the entire surface of the quilt. Quilting shrinks the project and you want it to shrink consistently all over. See also "Machine Quilting" on page 58 and "Pressing and Squaring Up" on page 59 for further details.

"Little Redwood," 6½" x 10". Minimal painting is enhanced with heavy stitching.

Island Sunrise

THIS SCENE WAS INSPIRED BY GORGEOUS PHOTOS OF HAWAII TAKEN BY MY SON, DAN. THE BEAUTY OF A SUNRISE REMINDS ME OF THE DIVINE HANDIWORK ALWAYS EVIDENT IN OUR EVERYDAY LIVES, IF WE JUST TAKE THE TIME TO LOOK.

Finished quilt: 20" x 17"
Techniques: Painting, fusible appliqué, thread play
Skill level: Beginner

Materials

Yardage is based on 42"-wide fabric. Prewash the white background fabric and do not use any fabric softeners.

- ⅝ yard of white solid fabric for painted background
- ¼ yard *total* of assorted black prints for tree trunks and rocks
- ¼ yard of dark blue print for binding
- 1 yard of fabric for backing and sleeve
- ⅜ yard of dark green or black tulle
- 21" x 24" piece of batting
- Fabric paints (see box below)
- Painting supplies (see page 8)
- Freezer paper, foam core board, or other water barrier
- 12" x 14" piece of water-soluble stabilizer
- Threads for quilting and thread motifs
- ½ yard of 18"-wide paper-backed fusible web
- 5" or 7" flat embroidery hoop with pinch release
- Black Sharpie fine-point pen

PAINT COLORS
DecoArt SoSoft: Lamp Black, Wisteria (lavender), True Blue, Baby Blue Deep, Baby Pink Deep, Pistachio Green, Tangerine, Primary Yellow, and White Pearl

Cutting

From the white solid fabric, cut:
1 rectangle, 19" x 22"

From the dark blue print, cut:
2 strips, 2¼" x 42"

From the backing and sleeve fabric, cut:
1 rectangle, 21" x 24"
1 rectangle, 8½" x 21"

From the dark green or black tulle, cut:
1 rectangle, 12" x 14"

Painting the Background

Gather supplies and set up your workspace. Be sure to read "Let's Paint" on page 8 before you begin. Test your fabric and paints, referring to "Test Run" on page 10. Keep a scrap of fabric handy to use for testing colors and techniques.

1. Position the white 19" x 22" rectangle in front of you with a long edge toward you. Lightly draw the 17" x 20" finished-size rectangle on the fabric with a pencil. Mark reference points in the margins 7" up from the bottom on each side, just outside the drawn lines. This is the dividing line between sky and sea. Also mark 2½" from the bottom on the left and 2" from the bottom on the right; these marks will be the guidelines for the division between land and sea.

Island Sunrise, 20" x 17"—designed, painted, and quilted by Pat Durbin

2. Place the fabric on a piece of freezer paper, shiny side up, or other water barrier over a foam core board or other work surface. Spray the sky area with water to make it slightly damp.

3. Squeeze out a ½" blob of several paint colors onto your paint palette. I used True Blue, Baby Blue Deep, Wisteria, Baby Pink Deep, Primary Yellow, and Tangerine. You may lighten colors by mixing with White if desired.

4. Pick up a little paint with a wet natural sponge and apply to the fabric using horizontal motions. Refer to the quilt photograph above for color placement or use your own idea of what the sunrise would look like. I wanted a bright spot where the sun was coming up and put that just to the right of the center above the water line. Then I added other colors and touches of yellow here and there. I put darker blue toward the top where the light had not yet reached the darkened sky. You can use the same sponge for each color, adding and blending the colors as you go. If necessary, rinse the sponge in water to remove some of the paint, and then continue.

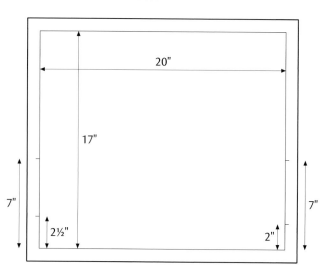

Partial horizon line painted

Painted sample ready for quilting

5. Look at the result. Do you need to add some more streaks of color? Do so now, and then let the piece dry.

6. To maintain the horizon line and make sure there is contrast between the sky and sea, paint a darker value along the horizon. Using a ruler or a piece of freezer paper as a guide, paint a straight horizon line on *dry* fabric using a *dry* tapered or flat brush and *undiluted* blue or blue green paint. Lift the ruler away, and use the brush to pull the paint down from the horizon about ½". Refer to the photograph above. Add more paint to your brush as needed. Let dry.

7. Protect the painted area with a piece of freezer paper laid lightly over the sky and horizon line, matte side down. Spray the area below the horizon line with water to dampen, and then move the paper out of the way. Paint the sea area similar to the sky using a wet sponge on wet fabric. Use several colors, such as True Blue, Pistachio Green, Wisteria, and Baby Pink Deep, blending them a

bit. Add a few reflections of the sun using Primary Yellow. Blend some White Pearl into the colored area as desired to add sparkle.

8. With a dry brush, carefully blend the wet sea paint into the lower portion of the dry horizon line paint. Do not get too close to the horizon line; the watery paint might bleed through to the sky.

9. Using Lamp Black and the 2½" mark as a starting point, paint an uneven area at the bottom for rocks and sand using a wet brush. It will bleed into the water a bit, but that is fine. It will also lighten as it dries, making it look more like sand. Let dry.

10. Check the horizon line. If needed, use undiluted paint on a dry brush on the dry painting to redraw the line; then brush to blend into the existing paint. Add any other touches that you would like, and then let everything dry again.

Quilting

Press the painting from the wrong side with a warm iron to flatten it. Place the fabric over batting and backing; baste, and then quilt the piece using free-motion designs of your choice. Be sure to refer to the labels for the brand of paint you are using. Some paints need to be heat set. If yours do, follow the manufacturer's instructions.

> **QUILT FIRST, PLANT LATER**
> I quilt my pieces before adding trees or other appliqués so that the horizontal quilting lines will go behind the tree shapes. This makes for easier quilting, and I like the look.

Adding the Fusible Appliqué

1. Trace the appliqué patterns for the tree trunks and rocks (pages 20 and 21) onto the paper side of your fusible web. Leave at least $1/2$" between the designs.

2. Using an iron and following the manufacturer's instructions, press the designs onto the wrong side of the chosen dark print scraps. You can use just one fabric or more for variety. Let the fabrics cool.

3. Carefully cut on the drawn line for each design. Peel away the paper and place the tree trunks and rocks on the quilted top. Refer to the project photo for placement or rearrange to please your eye. When satisfied with your arrangement, press to fuse.

4. With dark thread or smoke monofilament, zigzag or blanket stitch around the edges of the appliqué pieces.

5. Apply a small amount of black paint to a dry brush and, using a light touch, add a shadow extending from the bottom of each of the tree trunks, away from the sun toward the edge of the quilt.

Making and Adding the Palm Fronds

1. Using a permanent pen, trace the outlines of the palm frond patterns on page 21 onto a piece of water-soluble stabilizer. Also draw in the center vein in each frond. Keep a margin of about 2" around and between the designs, and do not cut them apart.

2. Place the tulle on top of the stabilizer and pin the corners together. Center one of the designs in the flat embroidery hoop, using the pinch release to tighten and hold the tulle and stabilizer. Smooth and stretch out fullness within the hoop. Remove the pins as you secure the design with stitching or if they're in the way of the hoop.

3. Set up your sewing machine for free-motion sewing. Thread your machine with dark thread in the bobbin and on top. Drop the feed dogs (or cover them) and put on a darning or free-motion foot. Set the stitch on zigzag with a width slightly less than $1/8$". You can widen the zigzag as you get used to the method if you desire.

4. Align the hoop so that a center vein of one of the palm fronds is horizontal. Begin at the center and sew along the vein of the branch with a horizontal movement. Turn the hoop as needed to follow the center vein line. Travel back along the branch to the center where you started. If needed, you can stop, undo the hoop, and reposition it along the design using the pinch release.

5. Turn the hoop so that you can sew at an angle away from the center vein and back up using back-and-forth motions, creating spiky-looking designs going from the center to the end and filling in the outline of the design. Vary the angle as you go. Turn the hoop as needed and stitch back toward the center of the palm along the other side of the vein, creating a sharper angle of

spines on the frond. The outline is only a guide. Use your judgment and artistic ability to make the fronds look the way you want.

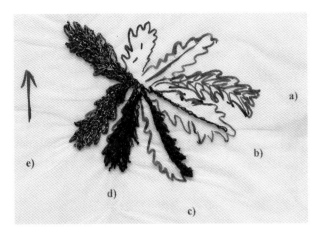

Example shows **a)** *blue ink indicating motion,* **b)** *stitched central vein,* **c)** *one side of fronds sewn,* **d)** *both sides sewn, and* **e)** *variegated green thread used.*

6. Repeat this thread play for each of the palm fronds. Vary the angles of the stitches and even change the thread for variety if desired.

7. Audition the tree top by taking it out of the hoop and putting it over the tree trunk on the quilt top to see how it looks. If desired, reinsert it in the hoop and add more thread.

8. Repeat the process to make the tops of the other palm trees in a similar manner.

9. When you're satisfied with the trees, refer to "Finishing the Thread Motifs" on page 13.

Completed palm tree top with partial trimming

10. Pin the palm fronds in place. Zigzag stitch them to the quilt sandwich with smoke monofilament for top thread. Stitch around the edges of the fronds to secure. You can also stitch the center of the branches if needed or desired.

Finishing the Quilt

1. Refer to "Pressing and Squaring Up" on page 59 to flatten and trim the quilt.

2. Sew the 2¼" binding strips together end to end and bind the quilt, referring to "Binding" on page 59.

3. Make a hanging sleeve, add a label, and hang your quilt. Refer to page 61 for detailed information.

4. Call all your quilting friends and celebrate!

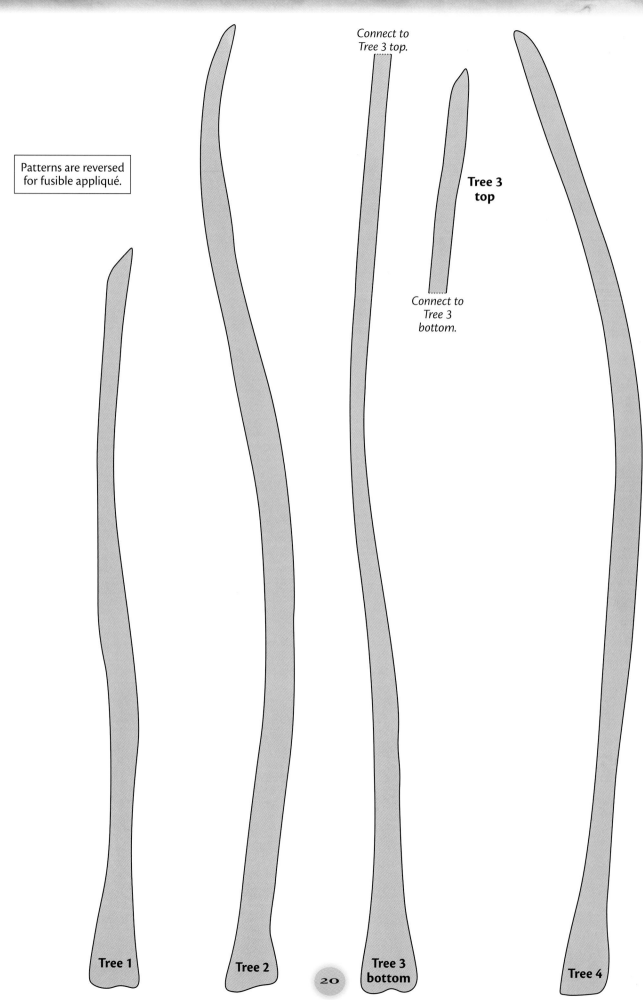

Patterns are reversed for fusible appliqué.

Tree 1

Tree 2

Connect to Tree 3 top.

Tree 3 top

Connect to Tree 3 bottom.

Tree 3 bottom

Tree 4

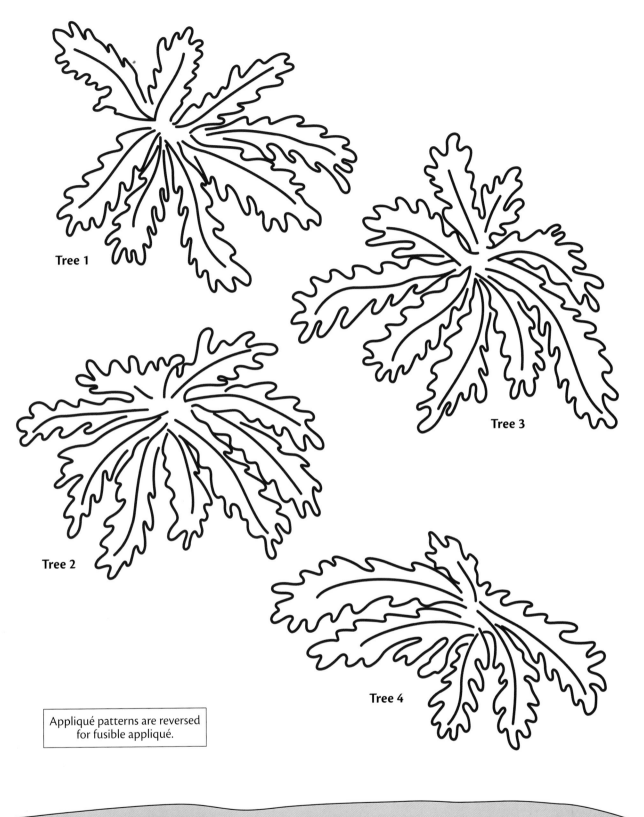

Tree 1

Tree 3

Tree 2

Tree 4

Appliqué patterns are reversed
for fusible appliqué.

Upper rocks

Lower rocks

Lacy Leaves Table Runner

THE BEAUTIFUL, NATURAL FORMS
OF LEAVES ADORN THIS LOVELY
ASYMMETRICAL TABLE RUNNER.
IT LOOKS COMPLEX BUT IS
ACTUALLY QUITE EASY TO MAKE.

Finished table runner: 12½" x 46"
Finished napkins: 17" x 17"
Techniques: Piecing, thread play
Skill level: Intermediate

Materials for Table Runner

Yardage is based on 42"-wide fabric.

¼ yard or 1 fat eighth *each* of 12 different white, off-white, and cream prints

1 yard of cream print for backing

⅜ yard of apple green print for accent and binding

⅜ yard of shiny apple green tulle

16" x 54" piece of batting

3 pieces, 12" x 12", of water-soluble stabilizer

Threads for quilting and thread motifs

5" or 7" flat embroidery hoop with pinch release

Black Sharpie fine-point pen

Materials for Four Napkins

1⅛ yards of apple green print

1⅛ yards of cream print

Freezer paper

Spray starch or sizing

Cutting for Table Runner

From *each* of the 12 white, off-white, and cream prints, cut:
1 rectangle, 4" x 18" (12 total)

From the apple green print, cut:
2 strips, 1¼" x 18"
4 binding strips, 2¼" x 42"

From the backing fabric, cut:
2 rectangles, 16" x 28"

From the tulle, cut:
3 squares, 12" x 12"

Piecing the Background

This is not a difficult pattern to sew; however, please read through all the instructions and study the diagrams before you begin.

1. Arrange the 4" x 18" cream and white rectangles in order from light to dark. All the pieces will be quite light, so this sorting is purely by relative values. Make six pairs of rectangles, with each pair containing a light print and a darker print.

2. Place the pieces right sides together, and sew together along one long edge. Press seam allowances open.

3. Arrange the six pairs as shown, alternating light and darker, and sew them together. When finished, you should have one long pieced section which consists of all 12 pieces and measures approximately 18" x 42". Press the seam allowances open.

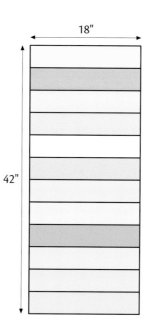

4. Fold the piece from step 3 in half so that it measures approximately 18" x 21". Align the seams with each other and use a ruler and rotary cutter to trim along one edge to straighten it, cutting it at a 90° angle to the seams.

5. From the just-straightened edge, cut six segments 2½" wide. Keep the horizontal lines of the ruler aligned with the seams so that your vertical cuts will be accurate. You will need six segments of the pieced strips.

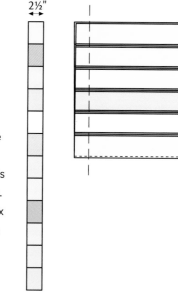

Cut 6 segments.

6. Lay the strips on an ironing board and number them 1 through 6. Rotate strips 2, 4, and 6 as shown to help mix up the fabrics.

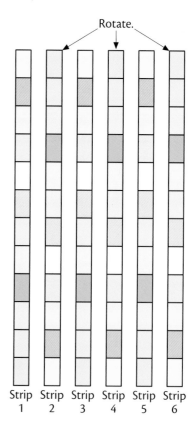

Rotate.

Strip 1   Strip 2   Strip 3   Strip 4   Strip 5   Strip 6

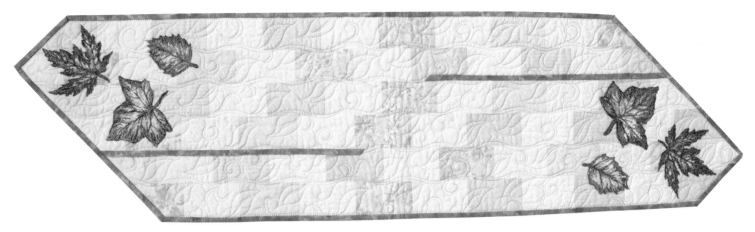

7. Group the strips into three sets: set A consisting of strips 1 and 2, set B consisting of strips 3 and 4, and set C consisting of strips 5 and 6. Stagger the placement of each set by a half rectangle as shown. Move strip 2 down a half rectangle; move strip 4 up a half rectangle; move strip 6 down a half rectangle. Pin each set with right sides together, and sew. Press the seam allowances in the direction of the arrows in the diagram.

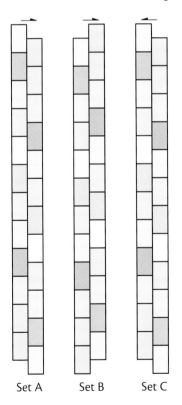

Set A   Set B   Set C

8. Fold each 1¼" green strip in half lengthwise, wrong sides together, and press to make the accent strips.

9. Place one green strip along the right side of set A, on strip 2, with raw edges aligned. Place the strip so that it ends about 16" from the top of the strip as shown. Insert a few pins to hold it in place. Place the second green strip along set C on strip 5 at the opposite end, about 16" from the end. Pin. Create diagonal ends by folding the strip under at a 45° angle so that all raw edges will be caught in the seam. Pin securely at the fold and along the edges.

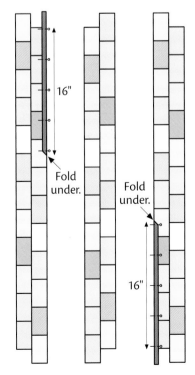

16"

Fold under.

Fold under.

16"

10. Referring to the diagram for staggering and placing the sets, pin and then sew the sets together. Press both seam allowances toward set B. This will allow the folded green accents to lie flat toward the outer edges of the table runner.

11. Place your patchwork on a flat surface so that you can mark the ends with a 6" x 24" ruler. Place the corner of your ruler in the middle of strip 5 and make sure the 45°-angle line is parallel to a lengthwise seam. Use a pencil or fabric marker to mark the cutting lines for the angled ends. Repeat for the opposite end, placing the corner of the ruler in the middle of strip 2. Do not cut yet; wait until after the quilting is complete.

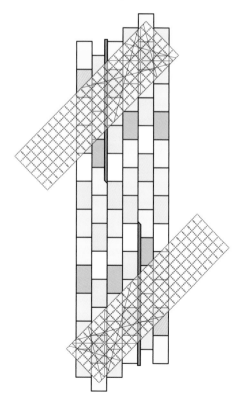

Quilting and Finishing

1. Sew the two backing rectangles together to form a 16" x 55$\frac{1}{2}$" rectangle; press the seam allowances open. Layer and baste the top, batting, and backing.

2. Quilt as desired. I used a vining leaf quilting pattern that travels the length of the quilt top, going right over the marked line at the ends. I avoided stitching on the green strips to keep them more dimensional.

3. Steam from the back when quilting is done. Check the markings again with your ruler to be sure your angles are OK and that the points are still positioned correctly. The quilting may have distorted this slightly. Cut away excess fabric along the marked lines using a ruler and rotary cutter.

4. Sew together the green binding strips and bind, referring to "Binding" on page 59. The unusual angles will work in a similar way to regular binding corners. Sew to where the $\frac{1}{4}$" seams will intersect, and then take a couple of backstitches. Cut the threads and remove the quilt from the machine. Fold back the binding to where the strip is aligned with the side you are going to stitch next. Then fold back down and pin, leaving a little tuck that will allow for folding a miter. Backstitch and continue sewing until the binding is complete.

Making the Leaves

1. Trace the leaf patterns on page 29 with a permanent pen onto a piece of water-soluble stabilizer. Include the veins. Trace two of each leaf design, keeping a margin of about 2" around and between the different designs. You should be able to fit two leaves on each piece of stabilizer.

2. Pin the corners of the tulle and water-soluble stabilizer together. Center one of the designs in the flat hoop, using the pinch release to tighten and hold the layers of tulle and stabilizer. Remove the pins as you secure with stitching or they get in the way of the hoop. Undo the hoop as needed and move it along the design using the pinch release. Smooth and stretch out any fullness with the hoop.

3. Thread the machine with 40-weight thread in the color of your choice in both the bobbin and on top.

4. Set up the machine for free-motion sewing by dropping (or covering) the feed dogs and attaching the darning foot or free-motion foot. Set the stitch on zigzag with a width slightly less than 1/8".

5. Align the hoop and turn as you need to in order to follow the lines. Begin at the outside edge and sew completely around the design, moving the hoop if needed. Go around again if needed to get a good edge. Stitch the main veins of the leaf in a similar manner. You can hold the edges of the hoop with your fingers to turn and maneuver it.

6. For the next round, use the same thread or change the color of the top thread if desired. Sew back and forth with lines horizontal to the edge stitching. Catch the sewn edge and extend toward the center of the leaf. Add some long and short lines of stitching, 1/2" to 1/4" from the edge. This makes a ragged edge. You may wish to do some of this type of stitching in the center area also. I didn't fill in the entire design, because I wanted the leaf to be lacy. I also wanted to be able to see the fabric through the leaf, but feel free to do as you wish.

ONE IS GOOD, MORE IS BETTER
I like to use at least three different shades of thread colors for each leaf to add depth and charm. Add a zinger, if you like—a bright color, a shiny rayon, or a variegated thread. All these options will make your leaves more interesting.

Edge of design complete, with interior partially sewn

7. Look at what you have. Do you want to change thread colors and enhance the motif some more? Do so now.

8. Repeat for other leaves in a similar manner, changing thread colors for variety.

9. When you are satisfied with the leaves, refer to "Finishing the Thread Motifs" on page 13.

10. Pin the leaves in place on the quilt top. Zigzag stitch to the quilt sandwich with clear monofilament for the top thread, and in the bobbin use thread that matches the back of the quilt. Stitch around the edges of the leaves and on some of the veins to secure.

Napkins

The following directions are for making one napkin. Repeat to make a set of four.

1. Cut two freezer-paper patterns, one 16" square and one 17" square. Use the lines on your rotary-cutting mat to make this easier.

2. With a dry iron, press the 16" freezer-paper square to the wrong side of the cream fabric, about 1" from the selvages and cut edges. Use the freezer paper as a guide to cut fabric with a ½" margin all around. You'll have a 17" x 17" square of fabric.

3. Brush the edge of the fabric that extends beyond the paper with sizing or spray starch that has been sprayed into a lid. Press each corner over the freezer paper at a 45° angle. Press all four sides over the pattern, keeping the corners sharp.

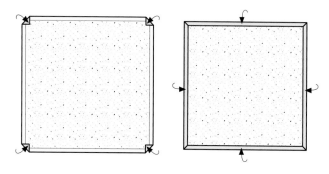

4. Press the 17" freezer-paper square onto the wrong side of the green fabric, about 1½" from the selvages and cut edges. Use the paper pattern as a guide to cut the fabric 1" larger all around. You'll have a 19" x 19" square of fabric.

5. Repeat step 3, pressing the 1" margin over the freezer-paper pattern.

6. Carefully remove the paper from each square. Place the green square right side down on the ironing board. Center the cream square right side up on top of the green square. The cream fold should cover the raw edge of the green border. Align the cream square so that all edges are equidistant from the green folded edge.

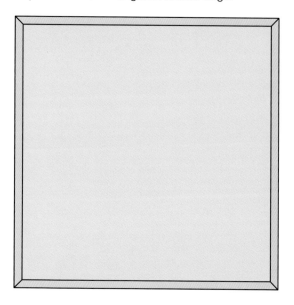

7. Pin in the center of the square, at the edges and corners, and at some places midway to hold securely for stitching.

8. Stitch with fancy thread and a wide decorative stitch of your choice, catching the folded edge of the cream fabric. Press with a warm iron.

Floral Palette

THE BEAUTY OF A FLOWER
INSPIRES AND WARMS THE
PAINTER'S SOUL. I WANTED
THE PAINTED BLOCKS TO
BE THE STAR OF THIS QUILT,
SO I CHOSE A VARIETY
OF ALMOST SOLIDS FOR
THE PATCHWORK BLOCKS.
THE COLORS ECHO THOSE
USED IN THE FLOWERS.

Finished quilt: 55½" x 66"
Finished block: 7½" x 7½"
Techniques: Piecing, dry-on-dry painting
Skill level: Intermediate

Materials

Yardage is based on 42"-wide fabric. Prewash the white fabric and do not use any fabric softeners.

- 1⅛ yards of red fabric for blocks and setting triangles
- ⅞ yard of white fabric for blocks
- ⅞ yard of dark blue print for border and binding
- ½ yard each of 3 different blue fabrics for blocks
- ½ yard each of 3 different green fabrics for blocks
- ¼ yard of turquoise fabric for blocks
- 3⅔ yards of backing fabric
- 60" x 70" piece of batting
- 18" x 26" piece of freezer paper or cellophane for water barrier and pattern duplication
- Black Sharpie fine-point pen
- Fabric paints (see box below)
- Painting supplies (see page 8)

PAINT COLORS
DecoArt SoSoft: Christmas Red, Baby Pink Deep, Hauser Dark Green, Avocado Green, Antique Gold, and Primary Yellow

Cutting

The cutting and piecing instructions are written so that the blues and greens will match in each individual block. If you want to make scrappy blocks, you don't have to worry about cutting matching pieces.

From the 3 blue fabrics, cut a total of:
14 strips, 3" x 42"; cut the strips into:
    36 squares, 3" x 3"*
    38 rectangles, 3" x 5½"*
    20 rectangles, 3" x 8*

From the 3 green fabrics, cut a total of:
14 strips, 3" x 42"; cut the strips into:
    38 squares, 3" x 3"**
    38 rectangles, 3" x 5½"**
    18 rectangles, 3" x 8"**

From the red fabric, cut:
2 strips, 3" x 42"; cut into 20 squares, 3" x 3"

5 squares, 12½" x 12½"; cut the squares twice diagonally to yield 20 side setting triangles (2 are extra)

2 squares, 6½" x 6½"; cut the squares once diagonally to yield 4 corner setting triangles

From the turquoise fabric, cut:
2 strips, 3" x 42"; cut into 18 squares, 3" x 3"

From the white fabric, cut:
2 strips, 3" x 42"; cut into 18 squares, 3" x 3"
1 rectangle, 20" x 28"

From the dark blue print, cut:
7 strips, 1½" x 42"
7 binding strips, 2¼" x 42"

Cut 18 pairs of matching 3" squares and 3" x 5½" rectangles for block B. Cut 20 pairs of matching 3" x 5½" and 3" x 8" rectangles for block A.

**Cut 20 pairs of matching 3" squares and 3" x 5½" rectangles for block A. Cut 18 pairs of matching 3" x 5½" and 3" x 8" rectangles for block B.*

Piecing Block A

Refer to the piecing diagram below, and press all seam allowances open.

1. Sew the red 3" squares to 20 green 3" squares, chain piecing them to make 20 sets. Press.

2. Sew a matching green 3" x 5½" rectangle to each unit from step 1, chain piecing them to make 20 units. Press.

3. Sew a blue 3" x 5½" rectangle to each unit from step 2, chain piecing to make 20 units. Press.

4. Sew a matching blue 3" x 8" rectangle to each unit from step 3, chain piecing to make 20 blocks. Press.

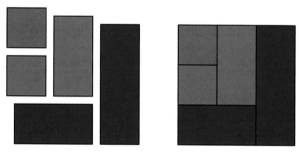

Block A.
Make 20.

Piecing Block B

To make block B, you will use the turquoise 3" squares, the blue 3" squares, the blue and the green 3" x 5½" rectangles, and the green 3" x 8" rectangles. Refer to the piecing diagram below and follow the steps for "Piecing Block A" to make 18 blocks.

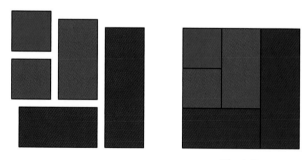

Block B.
Make 18.

Piecing Block C

1. Arrange three each of the blue, green, and white 3" squares in rows as shown. Sew the squares together into rows. Press seam allowances open.

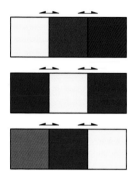

2. Matching the seams of the rows, pin and sew the rows together. Press seam allowances open.

3. Repeat to make six Nine Patch blocks.

Block C.
Make 6.

Painting Block D

Gather supplies and set up your workspace. Be sure to read "Let's Paint" on page 8 before you begin. Test your fabric and paints, referring to "Test Run" on page 10. Keep a scrap of fabric handy to use for testing colors and techniques. When painting these blocks, use dry fabric, a dry brush, and undiluted paint. Refer to the photograph on page 35 that shows the various stages of painting the flower. I suggest painting the blocks all at once in three sessions, allowing at least 20 to 30 minutes for each. First paint the flower petals, and then the leaves and stems; paint the flower centers and dots last.

1. With a black Sharpie marker, draw six 8" squares on the shiny side of the 18" x 26" piece of freezer paper (or cellophane), leaving a ½" margin between the squares as shown. This will become your pattern and it will also serve as a water barrier.

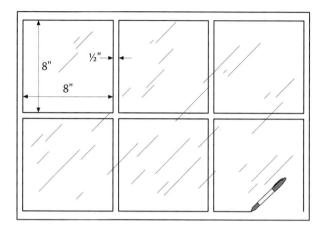

2. Center a square over the flower pattern on page 39 and trace the outline of the flower using the Sharpie marker; repeat for the six squares. Allow a few minutes for the ink to dry. Check it by wiping a scrap of light fabric over it.

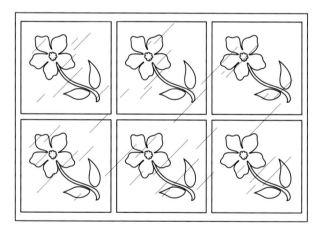

3. Place the 20" x 28" white rectangle over the pattern and pin the corners so they won't shift. You should be able to see the marked patterns through the white fabric. Use a graphite pencil to mark the fabric at the corners of each 8" square where the 8" square corners from the pattern show through. This will be a guide for cutting later.

4. Squeeze a small amount of Christmas Red paint onto your palette. Test the brush and paint on a scrap of fabric to get the feel for it.

5. Using a small, *dry* tapered brush, carefully paint the outside edge of all the flower petals. Leave a small section unpainted in the center of each petal and in the flower center. Set the brush aside on your palette to use for blending in step 7.

6. Squeeze some Baby Pink Deep paint onto your palette and use a small round, dry brush to fill in the center section of each petal in all of the blocks.

7. Using the brush set aside in step 5, brush and blend red paint into the pink. Add some lines that extend into the pink like thin veins in the petal, referring to the photograph. Repeat for all six flower blocks. Clean the brushes, and allow the paint to dry.

KEEP IT DRY

Remember, it is very important to use *dry* brushes for the flowers. If any water gets into the paint, the paint will bleed and won't make a distinct line.

8. Squeeze some Hauser Dark Green paint onto your palette. Use a dry tapered brush or small round brush to carefully paint the stem of each flower. Paint and fill in the leaves.

9. Squeeze out some Avocado Green. Using the same brush, add some highlights to each leaf. Blend as desired. Repeat for each flower block. Clean the brushes and allow the paint to dry completely.

10. Using a small round, dry brush, paint the flower centers with Antique Gold and let dry.

11. Using a tiny brush or a toothpick, add some Primary Yellow dots over the gold centers. Let dry.

12. Carefully cut out the 8" squares. (A square ruler, 8" x 8" or larger, is helpful for maintaining accuracy.) Use the marked pencil lines at the corners as a guide, but be sure that the flower is centered along the diagonal and that you have 8" on all sides. Cut away the extra fabric from the margins, first along the right and top edges. Then rotate the piece 180° and trim the remaining two sides.

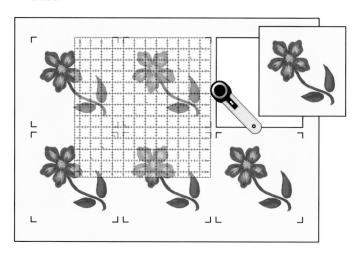

Assembling the Quilt Top

1. Referring to the assembly diagram below, lay out all blocks for the quilt top in diagonal rows. Notice that the red squares in the A blocks "kiss" in alternate rows, as do the turquoise squares in the B blocks. When the blocks are in position, place the setting triangles along the edges. Step back to see if the color placement is pleasing.

2. Sew the blocks into diagonal rows, matching and pinning seams where they meet. Press the seam allowances open.

3. Sew the rows together. Press the seam allowances open.

4. Because the setting triangles are cut slightly oversized, you will need to trim the edges of the quilt top before adding the border. Place the $\frac{1}{4}$" line of a long ruler along the points of the blocks; trim, leaving exactly $\frac{1}{4}$" beyond the points of the blocks for the seam allowance. Also trim the corner setting triangles, keeping the outside corner a true 90° angle.

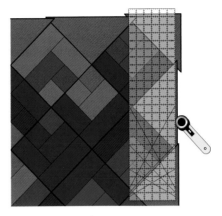

Trim ¼" from points.

Adding the Border

1. Sew the $1\frac{1}{2}$" dark blue strips together to make one long piece. Measure the width of the quilt through the center and use this measurement to cut the top and bottom borders.

2. Pin the border to the quilt at the block points and use care not to cut off the points when sewing. Sew the top and bottom borders. If you sew with the quilt on top, you'll be able to see the points. Press the seam allowances toward the border.

3. Measure the quilt through the center lengthwise, including the top and bottom borders just added. Use this measurement to cut the side borders. Pin and sew as before. Press the seam allowances toward the border.

Quilting and Finishing

1. Cut the backing fabric in half into two pieces, approximately 42" x 66". Sew the 66" edges together to make a backing with the seam running horizontally. Press the seam allowances open.

2. Referring to "Layering and Basting" on page 58, assemble the top, batting, and backing. Quilt as desired. I quilted my quilt in the following manner:

- I stitched in the ditch diagonally along the block seams using dark blue thread.

- I outline stitched the light squares ¼" from the seams, in a continuous manner vertically down the quilt.

- I free-motion quilted around each flower petal using decorative red thread, adding some details to enhance the flowers. I switched to a dark green thread and outlined the stems and leaves.

- I enlarged the flower design to use as a quilting pattern over blocks A and B.

- I stitched the remainder of the quilt, including the setting triangles, with meandering free-motion leaves.

3. Referring to "Binding" on page 59, add the 2¼" dark blue binding.

4. Please add a label; it's important.

Wonderland

WHEN WE VISITED
COLORADO ONE MAY,
IT WAS ABSOLUTELY
BEAUTIFUL. THE WEATHER
WAS MILD ENOUGH
TO ENJOY AND VIEW
THE LINGERING WINTER
SCENERY.

Finished quilt: 17" x 20"
Techniques: Painting, thread play
Skill level: Intermediate

Materials

Yardage is based on 42"-wide fabric. Prewash the white background fabric and do not use any fabric softeners.

- ⅔ yard of white solid fabric for painted background
- Scrap of dark brown fabric for tree trunks
- ⅓ yard of dark blue print for binding
- 1 yard of fabric for backing and sleeve
- ⅜ yard of light gray or light blue tulle
- 21" x 24" piece of batting
- 3 pieces, 12" x 16", of water-soluble stabilizer
- Fabric paints (see box at left)
- Painting supplies (see page 8)
- Freezer paper, foam core board, or other water barrier
- ¼ yard of paper-backed fusible web, 18" wide
- Threads for quilting and thread motifs
- 5" or 7" flat embroidery hoop with pinch release
- Black Pigma Micron pen 05 (optional)
- Black Sharpie fine-point pen

PAINT COLORS
DecoArt SoSoft: Lamp Black, Wisteria (lavender), True Blue, Baby Blue Deep, Hauser Dark Green, White, White Pearl, and Grey Sky. (Optional for painted rocks: Grey Sky, Pistachio Green, and Antique Gold.)

Cutting

From the white solid fabric, cut:

1 rectangle, 19" x 22"

1 square, 6" x 6" (optional rocks)

From the dark blue print, cut:

2 strips, 2¼" x 42"

From the backing and sleeve fabric, cut:

1 rectangle, 21" x 24"

1 strip, 8½" x 18"

From the light gray or blue tulle, cut:

3 pieces, 12" x 16"

Painting the Background

Gather supplies and set up your workspace. Be sure to read "Let's Paint" on page 8 before you begin. Test your fabric and paints, referring to "Test Run" on page 10. Keep a scrap of fabric handy to use for testing colors and techniques.

1. Position the white 19" x 22" rectangle in front of you on a flat surface so that the width is 19". Using a pencil, lightly draw the finished-size rectangle, 17" x 20". Mark reference points in the margins for the tree line. On the left, mark 9½" and 12" up from the bottom. On the right, mark 10½" and 14" up from the bottom.

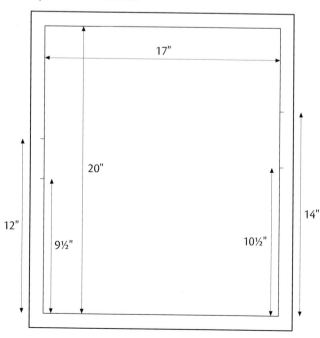

2. Cut a strip of freezer paper that is 18" long and approximately 2½" wide on the left side and 3½" wide on the right side. Press this to the background fabric, shiny side down, across the tree section. Covering this area will keep the fabric dry and help prevent the wet paint from seeping into it.

3. Place the fabric on your prepared water barrier, either a piece of freezer paper or cellophane over foam core board, table, or ironing board. Lightly spray the sky area with clean water to make it slightly damp.

4. Squeeze a ½" blob of each of the blue paint colors onto your palette. I used True Blue, Wisteria (lavender), and Baby Blue Deep. Lighten colors by mixing with White if desired.

5. Pick up a little paint with a wet natural sponge and apply it to the damp fabric using horizontal motions. Refer to the photographs on pages 43 and 45 for color placement guidance. I used True Blue in the upper-left corner, blending with Baby Blue Deep toward the right. As I worked my way down, I mixed in some of the Wisteria; toward the tree line I added Baby Blue Deep mixed with White. You can use the same sponge for each color, adding and blending the colors together as you go. (The sky may seep into the tree-line area under the freezer paper slightly, but that's OK. We'll cover it up later with trees.)

Note: I left a fist-sized area just left of the center without paint, as well as a couple of spots on the right. The wet blue paints will seep into these areas, making them look like clouds.

6. Look at the result. Add some more color if desired, and let dry.

7. You can leave the snow area white, or add some subtle shading with Grey Sky mixed with White Pearl. Add some water to the mixed paint and apply it to dampened fabric. To give the impression of a slight rise in the foreground, make a swooping motion with a sponge at an angle where you want the slope to be. You may rinse the sponge and add some White Pearl to other sections of the snow, just for a little glimmer. Let dry.

8. Clean your palette and sponge.

Painting the Trees

Paint the tree-line area with a dry brush or sponge onto dry fabric with undiluted paint. If any water is added to the mix, you won't get a distinct line. Refer to the photograph on page 45 for these steps.

1. Remove the freezer paper at the tree line. With Lamp Black paint on a tapered dry brush, paint a smooth line that curves gently across the entire width of the piece along the bottom of the tree line, using the pencil marks in the margin as guides. The spacing is approximate, so feel free to vary it. This line will define the difference between the snow and the tree line, so you want it to be smooth and distinct. Refer to section 1 of the photograph.

2. Using the brush, go back and increase the width of the line upward, so that you have about ½" to ¾" area painted. Refer to section 2 of the photograph. Let dry. Watch and *protect the bottom of this line* as you continue to paint in the next steps.

3. Switch to the dry natural sponge and dab Lamp Black paint along the rest of the tree line, making tree-like shapes. Refer to section 3 of the photograph. Carefully blend the trees into the top portion of the line created in step 2.

4. Pick up Hauser Dark Green alternately and dab some more, referring to section 4 of the photo. Cover most of the blank area and slightly onto the sky with spiky blobs. Some should be higher than others. You may let some white show through to simulate snow in a few areas around the trees. Remember that this is a distant view of trees and details are not necessary. You simply want to give the impression of trees.

5. When most of the area is covered, go back with the brush and stretch some of the paint up into the sky like the points of the trees, as in section 5 of the photograph. Add any other touches that you would like and then let the whole thing dry again. (Looks good, doesn't it?)

> **QUILT FIRST, PLANT LATER**
> I quilt my pieces before putting on the trees so that the horizontal quilting lines will go behind the tree shapes. This makes for easier quilting, and I like the look.

Quilting

1. Press the painting with a warm iron to remove wrinkles and smooth it out. Be sure to refer to your paint labels to see if your paints need to be heat-set. If they do, follow the manufacturer's instructions.

2. Place the fabric over the batting and backing; baste and quilt the piece using free-motion designs of your choice. Refer to section 6 of the photograph on page 45. I quilted in the following manner:

   Sky: I stitched free-form horizontal lines in the sky with a few stipples for clouds, and changed thread colors several times.

   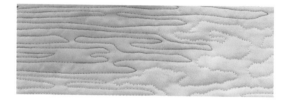

   Snow: I "drew" some hills with thread to divide the snow area. Then I filled in with echo quilting. This gives the look of drifted snow.

   Distant trees: I free-form quilted the background trees with a zigzag stitch, using a dark green variegated thread.

1   2   3   4   5   6

Various stages of the painting and quilting process

Making the Trees

1. Trace the pattern for tree 1 on page 48 onto a piece of water-soluble stabilizer with a permanent pen. Draw in the horizontal branches and a vertical middle line for reference. You need a margin of at least 2" around the design. Cut a piece of tulle the same size as the stabilizer.

2. Set up your sewing machine for free-motion sewing. Drop (or cover) the feed dogs and put on a darning or free-motion foot. Set the stitch on zigzag with a width slightly less than $1/8$". Use black thread in the bobbin and top.

3. Pin the corners of the tulle and stabilizer together. Align and fasten the hoop so that the bottom-left portion of the tree is in the center. Turn the hoop so that the trunk of the tree is crosswise to you.

4. Refer to the photograph below for the type of stitching done in each round. Each round will add color and fill in the bushiness of the tree.

Round 1: Stitch the tree skeleton and dark shadows using black thread. Begin at the bottom center and sew to the left, following the branch outline. Make a few small secondary branches on each main branch. Stitch back toward the center, move up the trunk to the next branch, and repeat the process. Experiment with turning the hoop at a different angle to see what style of stitch looks good to you. Stitch branches all the way up the left side, and back down the right to create the dark tree skeleton.

Notice the rounds of stitching:
    Round 1 *in the lower left,*
    Round 2 *in the upper left,*
    Round 3 *in the upper right, and*
    Round 4 *in the lower right.*

5. **Round 2:** Switch thread colors—maybe use a dark green on top and gray in the bobbin. Repeat the stitching process to add more branches between the ones that are already there. Begin at the bottom; stitch up the left side, and down the right. Fill in more of the area near the trunk in the middle, referring to the illustration. Try to stitch next to the previous stitching rather than directly on top.

6. **Round 3:** Switch thread colors again, maybe using a variegated green on top and a bright green in the bobbin or other colors of your choice. Add more branches and travel from the lower left up to the top and back down the right. Fill in more of the area in the middle, near the trunk. Try not to completely cover the stitches you've already made; you want the variety of colors to show. Make a branch in a couple of places that droops down over the next layer of the tree to add a more realistic look.

7. Look at the results and see if you need to add more thread color or density anywhere. You can lay the tree over the background to see how it looks.

8. **Optional Round 4:** Add highlights if desired. In the photograph at left, I used a variegated rust/gray/white for the top thread. I think it adds a little zing to the appearance.

9. Repeat the process to make the other trees in a similar manner. Tree 2 uses the same pattern but a different combination of colors. You could make it just a bit taller or shorter. Just a couple of different threads will make the tree distinct from the first one. Trees 3 and 4 are small and can both be put on the same piece of stabilizer. They were done with only one round of thread, but I filled them in more as I went along.

10. When you're satisfied with the trees, refer to "Finishing the Thread Motifs" on page 13.

Making the Tree Trunks

1. Using the tree trunk appliqué patterns on page 49, trace the designs onto the paper side of the fusible web. Leave at least ½" of space between the designs.

2. Using a hot iron, and following the manufacturer's instructions, press the designs onto the wrong side of the dark brown scraps. Let the fabrics cool.

3. Carefully cut on the drawn line for each design. Peel away the paper.

Place and Attach the Trees

1. Refer to the project photo on page 43 for placement of the trees and trunks, or arrange them to please your eye. Position the trunks under the appropriate trees. Place a pin in the top of the tree tops to hold them in place, and then flip them up and out of the way to avoid touching them with the iron. *A hot iron will damage your thread pieces.*

2. Fuse the trunks with your iron. Flop the trees back down and use pins to hold them in place.

3. Zigzag stitch the thread tree to the quilt sandwich with smoke monofilament for top thread. Stitch around the edges of the tree and travel down some of the branches to secure. This will puff up some of the branches for a more realistic look. Stitch the edges of the fused tree trunks below the trees.

4. Take a little Lamp Black paint on a dry brush using a light touch; extend a shadow from the bottom of the tree trunks, as shown. The imaginary sun is in the upper-right corner just off the quilt, so the shadows are below and slightly to the left of the trees.

Optional Painted Rocks

1. Place the 6" x 6" white square over the rock pattern on page 49. Use a black Pigma pen to trace directly onto the fabric.

2. Place this piece on your water barrier and use a fine, dry paintbrush to go over those lines with Lamp Black paint. Let dry.

3. Fill in the rocks with Grey Sky, Pistachio Green, or Antique Gold, referring to the quilt photograph above. Mix colors on some of the rocks.

4. While the paint is still wet, mix Lamp Black with a drop of water and use this to add shadows near the bottom-left edge of each rock. It will mix a bit with the colors already there for a natural look. Let dry.

5. Press fusible web to the wrong side of the completed rock painting and, when cool, trim around the group of rocks, leaving a ¼" seam allowance along the left and bottom margin. Remove the paper backing and place at the bottom corner of the quilted piece; fuse in place. Sew around individual rocks with smoke monofilament or black thread to secure the edges, outline rocks, and to add dimension.

Finishing the Quilt

1. Refer to "Pressing and Squaring Up" on page 59 to flatten and trim the quilt.

2. Sew the 2¼" binding strips together end to end and bind the quilt, referring to "Binding" on page 59.

3. Make a hanging sleeve, add a label, and hang your quilt. Refer to page 61 for detailed information.

Trees 1 and 2

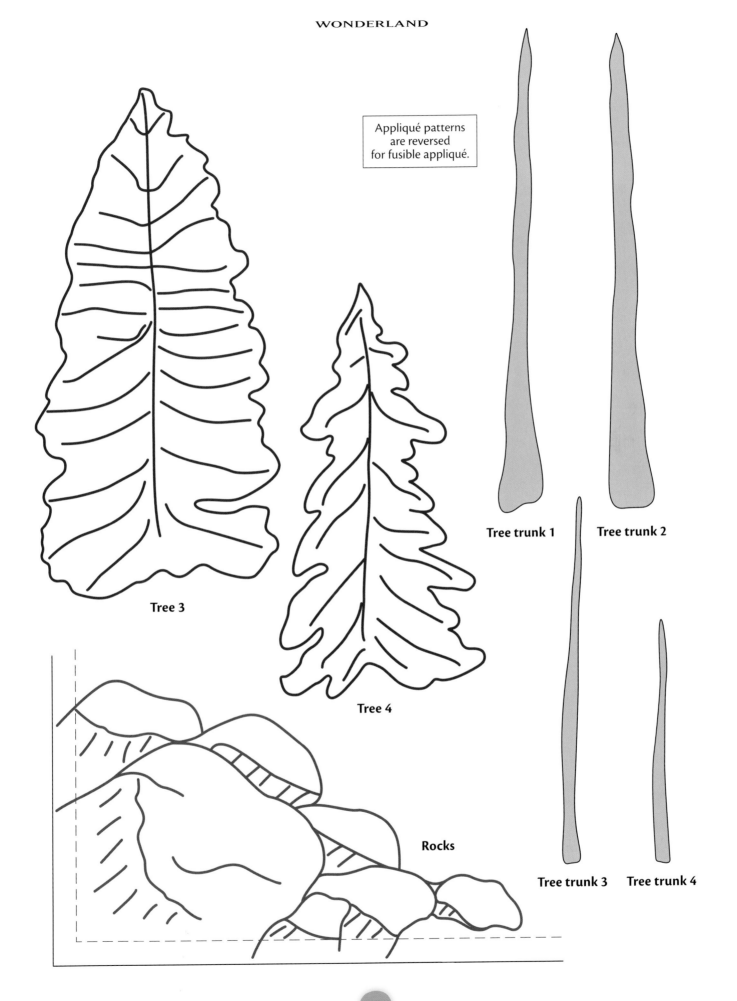

Appliqué patterns are reversed for fusible appliqué.

Tree trunk 1

Tree trunk 2

Tree 3

Tree 4

Tree trunk 3

Tree trunk 4

Rocks

Lakeside

STOP ALONG THE ROAD AND
STEP DOWN TO THE LAKE. FEEL
THE GENTLE BREEZE AND ENJOY
THE RESPITE FROM TRAVEL.

The instructions for this quilt assume that you've tried the painting techniques with one of the other projects and that you now have a feel for what paint will do on a damp piece of fabric. You've learned that to get a line to stay where you want it, you must use dry brush and dry fabric. You've also become more comfortable with blending colors.

So we now move on to a little more challenging piece. I've provided basic instructions and you'll need to add your own artist's interpretation as you go. Use my quilt as a reference when placing your colors in the different areas.

Finished quilt: 22" x 34"
Techniques: Painting, heavy quilting
Skill level: Intermediate

Materials

Yardage is based on 42"-wide fabric. Prewash the white background fabric and do not use any fabric softeners.

- $7/8$ yard of white solid fabric for painted background
- $1/4$ yard of light blue print for binding
- $1/8$ yard of dark print for flange (optional)
- $1\frac{1}{8}$ yards of fabric for backing and hanging sleeve
- 24" x 36" piece of batting
- Fabric paints (page 52)
- Painting supplies (page 8)
- Freezer paper or wide clear cellophane
- Foam core board (optional)
- Black Sharpie fine-point pen
- Black Pigma Micron pen 05
- Bottom Line thread for quilting (optional)

PAINT COLORS

DecoArt SoSoft: Hauser Dark Green, Avocado Green, Pistachio Green, Green Apple, Antique Gold, Warm Neutral, Buttermilk, Grey Sky, Lamp Black, Wisteria (lavender), Baby Blue Deep, Dark Chocolate, Burnt Sienna, White, and White Pearl

Cutting

From the white solid fabric, cut:
1 rectangle, 24" x 36"

From the dark print, cut:
3 strips, 1" x 42"

From the light blue print, cut:
3 strips, 2⅜" x 42"

From the backing and sleeve fabric, cut:
1 rectangle, 24" x 36"
1 strip, 8½" x 23"

Painting the Background

Gather supplies and set up your workspace. Be sure to read "Let's Paint" on page 8 before you begin. Test your fabric and paints, referring to "Test Run" on page 10. Keep a scrap of fabric handy to use for testing colors and techniques. Note that the sun position is high in the sky and slightly behind the trees.

1. Enlarge the pattern on page 57 by 375% (or to the size of your choice) to create a painting outline map.

2. Use either freezer paper or cellophane to create a water barrier, as described below.

   Freezer paper. Cover the enlarged painting map with freezer paper, shiny side up, and pin at the corners. Use a Sharpie fine-point permanent pen to trace the lines of the map onto the freezer paper. You can then put away the photocopy. The freezer paper will also serve as your water barrier.

   Cellophane. Cover the enlarged painting map and pin at the corners. You will be able to see the lines through the cellophane and it will also be the water barrier.

3. Position the white 24" x 36" fabric rectangle over the painting map and pin it to the freezer paper or cellophane at the corners and in the middle of the long edges in the margin. You should be able to see the dark lines through the white fabric. With the Pigma pen, trace the outlines of the painting map directly onto the fabric and make a small

LAKESIDE

dot at each corner for reference. The markings will provide guidelines for painting the various features. The outlines will be covered with paint or thread, and because they are fine lines, they will not interfere with your art piece. Just be sure the ink has dried before you spray with water.

4. Place the fabric and water barrier on a foam core board or directly on a table or ironing board for painting. You may need to let the fabric drape off the edge of the table to reach some areas as you work. Lightly spray the sky area with clean water to make it slightly damp. Leave the tree-line area blank at this point. (The sky paints may seep into it slightly, but we'll cover that up with trees later.)

5. Squeeze out a blob of the sky paint colors onto your paint palette. I used Baby Blue Deep and White. I lightened the blue toward the bottom of the sky by mixing with White. Use a wet sponge and horizontal motions, blending and covering the entire sky section. Refer to the quilt photograph on page 53 for color placement. You can use the same sponge for each color, adding and blending the colors as you go. Look at the result. Add some more color if desired. Let dry.

6. Spray the lake water area with water and use Baby Blue Deep mixed with a little water to cover the whole area for the lake. Then blend other colors into this base. Along the top right of the lake area, I mixed Wisteria with the blue and made some uneven passes with the sponge. Next I added Avocado Green and blended it into most of the rest of the water, leaving some horizontal lighter areas. Along the left shore I mixed in some Burnt Sienna. From the top of the water extending down quite a way is a reflection of the trees. Use Hauser Dark Green to create and blend in those vague shapes. The trees are actually blocking the sunlight, so the left side of the water needs to be darker than the rest. Take a little Lamp Black paint on a brush and lightly outline the edge of the water all along the shoreline. Use White on the sponge and highlight sunlit water, then pick up some White Pearl and just touch and blend it here and there for a little shimmer. Now take a look. Wasn't that easy?

Note: Water will reflect the colors around it; adding those colors to the water will make it look more realistic.

7. When all paint has dried, use Burnt Sienna, Buttermilk, Warm Neutral, Grey Sky, and Dark Chocolate in differing mixes to cover the sandy shore area. Cover the areas between and underneath the trees. Notice the light spots and try to duplicate them. Toward the bottom of the piece in the left foreground, spray the area with water and apply a light coat of Burnt Sienna with a wet sponge, making some areas darker than others. As it dries it will resemble sand.

8. Use Dark Chocolate mixed with Lamp Black on a brush to paint the tree trunks, with some of them extending up into the trees. Let dry.

9. Notice the trees that are mostly black; paint these first with a dry natural sponge. Add greens, alternating the colors and mixing in black where the darker areas show. As the trees dry, you can pick up a different shade to add over the previous paint layer and highlight certain areas such as the tips of the branches. This allows the tree color underneath to show through. The little trees in front are a lighter, brighter color. I mixed Green Apple with Avocado Green and used a light touch. This color combination can also be used to create the grassy area on the left of the shore and foreground. Use the sponge to dab on color in those areas.

10. To create the distant mountain, brush in Grey Sky mixed with Lamp Black. Paint the closer sliver of land with Lamp Black.

11. Use Grey Sky, White, and Lamp Black to dab tiny rocks over the sand along the distant shore. The larger rocks in the foreground can be the same colors, with a touch of Antique Gold or one of the green shades. Shadows fall to the left and bottom.

12. Fill the right side of the foreground with a dry sponge and Pistachio Green; mix in Avocado Green and Hauser Dark Green for the bushy weeds. Refer to the quilt photograph on page 53. Apply color to other grassy or bushy areas that need some green. Let dry.

Tree line

13. Check for any additions you want to make to the trees, water, rocks, or shoreline.

14. With Dark Chocolate, Lamp Black, and a highlight of Antique Gold, use a dry brush to carefully paint the tall dry weeds. Let dry.

15. Brush on the driftwood and branches with White, Grey Sky, and Lamp Black. Add more limbs if you desire. The branches are white on the tops with black underneath where the shadow falls.

16. After all the paint has dried, you can add details with more paint or with fabric-marking pens.

Quilting

1. Press the painting with a warm iron to remove wrinkles and smooth it out. Be sure to refer to your paint labels to see if your paints need to be heat-set. If they do, follow the manufacturer's instructions.

2. Place the fabric over the batting and backing; baste and quilt the piece using free-motion designs of your choice. Quilt to enhance the picture. For this type of quilt, I quilt densely, using the Bottom Line thread in the bobbin. It enables me to quilt more heavily without distorting the shape of the quilt. I use straight stitching as well as

zigzag stitching for trees and bushes. You can quilt as you like, but I like to add quilting that enhances the realism of the picture. Here's what I did:

Sky and water: I quilted free-form horizontal lines in the sky and similar lines for the water, changing thread colors frequently to help enhance the colors.

Trees: I quilted the trees with a free-form zigzag stitch, using first black and then several different green threads.

Sand: I followed the contours of the sand or dirt and, where there are rocks, outlined them with thread.

Grass: I used long, spiky back-and-forth motions, turning the zigzag stitch on again for a bushy effect.

Large brown weeds: I outlined with black and made the lines uneven as I followed the stems down to the ground.

Dead branches: I outlined the branches that are large enough to follow and added a few little off shoots here and there.

3. Fill in any areas that need more quilting to balance the stitching throughout.

Finishing the Quilt

1. Refer to "Pressing and Squaring Up" on page 59 to press the quilt. Allow to dry.

2. Turn the quilt over and square the top to 22" x 34" by trimming the edges. Remember the reference dots. That is where your corners should be—adjust as needed. A 12½" square ruler is helpful to get corners square. Check the width in several places to see if all the measurements are the same. Check the length, too, and correct any problems.

3. **Optional flange:** This is an optional strip, sometimes called a flat piping, that provides another opportunity to add a touch of color or design. Cut the 1" x 42" strips to fit each side of your quilt. Fold the four strips in half lengthwise, wrong sides together, and press. With the quilt flat on an ironing board, align the raw edges of two of the folded strips with the raw edges of the sides of the quilt. Pin securely and sew with a scant ¼" seam. Repeat to add the top and bottom flange pieces.

4. Sew the 2⅜" binding strips together end to end and bind the quilt, referring to "Binding" on page 59. Use a ¼" seam allowance, and the stitching line of the flange will be hidden.

5. Make a sleeve and hand stitch it to the backing along the top of the quilt. Refer to page 61.

6. Make a label and hand stitch it to the bottom of the backing.

Aren't you proud? If you want to send or email a picture of the finished quilt to me, I'd be so happy to see it. (See "About the Author" on page 63.)

Painting outline guide
Enlarge pattern 375%.

Quiltmaking Basics

REVIEW THIS SECTION
FOR BASIC INFORMATION ON
PIECING, PRESSING,
AND FINISHING YOUR
PICTURE QUILT.

Piecing

For pieced projects, the most important key for success is to cut your pieces accurately, and piece them with an exact ¼" seam. If you don't, you'll be struggling all the time to match things up.

Pressing

Most quilters press seam allowances to one side. I prefer to press the seam allowances open when possible. This results in a flat, smooth surface on the quilt top. It makes quilting over seams much easier and I think it makes matching seams easier as well. Press all the seam allowances open from the back of a block; then turn it over and press the seam from the front to flatten it.

Layering and Basting

The three layers of the quilt are the backing, batting, and pieced top or painted picture. You may hand baste these layers together with needle and thread, pin baste with safety pins, or use basting spray. Before basting, press the backing fabric to remove any wrinkles.

Batting is your choice; however, I like cotton batting by the Warm Company. I make a lot of wall hangings and this batting is stable and resists stretching.

Temporary Spray Basting

This is the method I use most often, especially for larger quilts. If your quilt is large, ask someone to help you and be sure to use basting spray in a well-ventilated room.

1. Lay the backing right side down and tape the corners to the table.

2. Cover the exposed table area with paper to protect from overspray.

3. Lay the batting on top of the backing and smooth it out.

4. Lay the picture or pieced quilt top on top of both.

5. Fold back half of the quilt top, spray the batting, and lay the top back down. Try to avoid wrinkles, and then gently pat the surface. Repeat with the other half of the quilt top.

6. Fold back half the batting and quilt top (they are stuck together now), spray the backing, and lay the top two layers back down. Pat the surface and repeat for the other half of the quilt.

Machine Quilting

Straight-line quilting may be done with a walking foot attached to your sewing machine or a built-in dual-feed system. Either mechanism feeds all three layers of the quilt sandwich under the needle evenly to prevent them from shifting. For curves and wavy lines you need a free-motion foot, sometimes called a darning foot. With this method you drop the feed dogs (or cover them) and guide the quilt sandwich under the needle with your hands. The machine does not move the fabric at all.

Most of my quilting is done in a free-motion style. I can move the quilt around in any direction to enhance the quilted piece. It is kind of like sketching. This is also the method I use for thread play. Choose threads to enhance the picture.

Always test your threads and tension before working on a quilt. Keep a practice "throwaway" sandwich near your machine for this purpose.

Try to keep an even amount of stitching over the entire surface of the quilt. This prevents one section from drawing up more than another. Try to use designs that enhance your picture, such as swirls in an area that represents water or waves, leaves on floral areas, and stippling in the clouds. Use your imagination and have fun.

Pressing and Squaring Up

After the quilting is finished, the quilt may be a little out of square and sometimes will ripple, especially with heavy quilting or threadwork. To flatten the quilt, turn your piece face down on your ironing surface. (This protects any thread motifs from the iron.) Spray the back with water, and then use a hot, dry iron to press and flatten it. Lay it flat, face down, to dry completely.

To square up the quilt, place it on a rotary-cutting mat right side up. Trim the top two corners and top edge first, using a square at the corners so they will be 90°. Measure down from the top line in equal distances from the center and edges to mark the bottom edge lightly with a pencil or other fabric marker. A good check is to measure from the top-left corner to the bottom-right corner. Check the opposite diagonal to see if the measurement is the same. They should match if the quilt is square. Check the width in a couple of places to make sure you trim them correctly. Trim the bottom and side edges and square the corners.

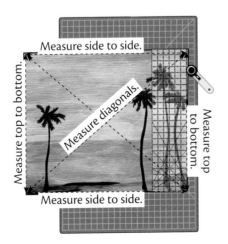

Measure side to side.
Measure top to bottom.
Measure diagonals.
Measure top to bottom.
Measure side to side.

Binding

For binding, multiply both the length and width of the quilt by two, and then add those numbers together for the total distance around the quilt; add about 12" extra for joining strips and mitering corners. For example, a 20" x 25" project needs (20" x 2) + (25" x 2) + 12", or 102". If you cut 40"-long strips across the fabric width, you'll need three strips for this example. Cut your binding strips $2\frac{1}{4}$" wide, or $2\frac{3}{8}$" if you've used a flange or flat piping.

1. Sew the binding strips right sides together at the ends diagonally, to make one long strip. Trim the excess fabric, leaving a $\frac{1}{4}$" seam allowance, and press the seam allowance open.

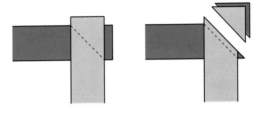

2. Press the strip in half lengthwise, with wrong sides together and raw edges aligned.

3. Unfold the binding at one end and turn under the beginning edge at a 45° angle as shown; press. Unfold and trim $\frac{1}{4}$" away from the pressed fold. Refold this $\frac{1}{4}$"-wide edge.

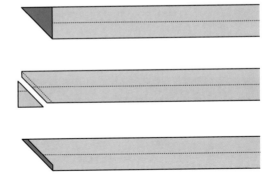

4. Refold the binding strip lengthwise, wrong sides together. Place the binding on the right side of the quilt sandwich about a third of the way up from the bottom corner. Place the quilt on an ironing board and pin the first side, pinning about every 6", aligning the raw edges with the raw edge of the quilt. Doing this on the board helps prevent stretching the edge. Sew to the quilt using a ¼" seam allowance. (If you have put on a flange, this sewing should cover the seam of the flange.) Stop sewing ¼" from the corner and backstitch a few stitches.

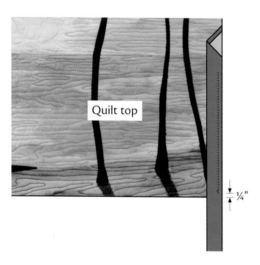

5. Remove the quilt from the sewing machine and clip the threads. Turn the quilt 90° so that you will be sewing along the next side. Fold the binding up and away from the quilt, creating a 45° angle. Fold the binding back down, lining it up with the next edge of the quilt. Pin the fold, and then pin the binding to the next side of the quilt as you did before.

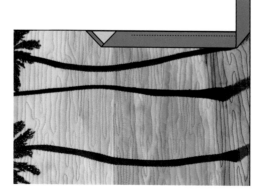

6. Begin with a backstitch and sew from the beginning edge of the quilt all along the next side; stop when you are ¼" from the next corner, backstitch, and repeat the mitering process. When you have done all the sides in this manner, overlap the end of the binding over the diagonal starting point and cut off, leaving about 1" extra. Trim this after you make sure you have enough to tuck into the pocket left from the beginning 45° edge.

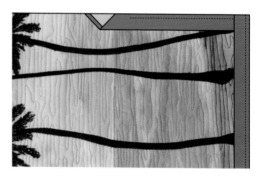

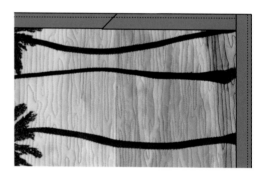

7. Check to make sure that all your corners look good. Then wrap the folded edge of the binding around to the back of the quilt and blind stitch it in place by hand so that it covers the machine stitching line. Fold mitered corners on the back side in the opposite direction from how you folded

them on the front to reduce bulk. Also stitch the beginning diagonal fold over the end of the binding.

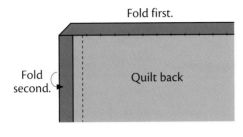

Fold first.

Fold second.

Quilt back

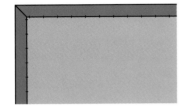

Hanging Sleeve

A hanging sleeve will help you to display your quilt nicely on the wall. These instructions will give you a hanging sleeve that is 4" wide when finished.

1. Cut a strip of fabric 8½" wide and 1" longer than the width of the finished quilt top. Turn under ½" on one end and press. Turn under ½" again and press. Repeat on the other end.

2. Stitch the hem on each end by machine. This is a nice place to use some of the fancy stitches on your machine, if you wish.

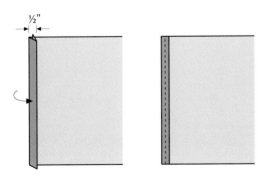

½"

3. Fold the fabric in half lengthwise, *wrong* sides together, and stitch using a ¼" seam allowance. Press the seam allowance open, and then shift it to the center of the sleeve and press the folds of the hanging sleeve. (The raw edges of the seam

allowances will be against the back of the quilt and the inside of the tube will have the finished seam.)

4. Pin the top edge of the sleeve just below the edge of the stitched binding, or approximately ½" from the edge of the quilt. Keep it a consistent distance. Pin the bottom edge loosely at the bottom fold. Hand stitch along the top and bottom, and stitch the back sides of the ends, leaving the tube open. Be careful to catch only the backing of the quilt sandwich.

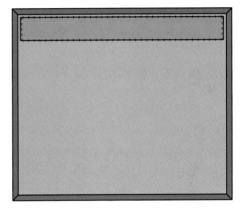

Signature Label

A signature label is important to document your quilt. It can be simple or elegant. Quilts last a long time, so add a label to tell people what you had in mind when you made this work of art. Include at least the following basic information:

- Your first and last name
- City and state where you live
- Date of completion

Other information could include:

- A credit if you've used someone's pattern, noting the designer and the book or magazine it came from.
- Sentiments or verses; I like to include a Bible verse.
- To and From information, along with the occasion, if the quilt is made for a gift.

When I design a label on my computer, I use a large font for the important information and a smaller font for the details. Paint a little scene if you want. Here's what I did for "Island Sunrise."

Displaying Your Quilt

Quilts add a warm touch wherever you hang them. Many of these quilts are like fine art, so my advice is to enjoy them as much as possible. To hang your quilt, slip your choice of hanging device through the sleeve and attach it to the wall. Here are some ideas:

- Curtain rods
- Wooden dowel rods
- Commercial quilt hangers

Think about where you will hang your quilts, keeping in mind that direct sunlight will damage or fade the colors over time. Minimize damage and rotate quilts frequently.

Small quilts can also be framed. You can do it yourself, or take them to a professional framer. Be sure to use spacers to provide air space between the fabric and the glass.

Tips for Cleaning and Washing

Most of the time a wall hanging can simply be shaken out to remove dust. When it becomes necessary to wash your quilt, please be gentle with it. Use a mild soap or detergent, and stand guard by the washer to keep it from agitating.

1. Fill the washer with tepid water and dissolve the detergent in the water.

2. Stop the action, add and submerge the quilt, and let soak for a few minutes.

3. Use your hands to agitate and squeeze to wash out dirt.

4. Set the washer to the spin cycle and let it spin out the water.

5. Stop the action, set the washer to the rinse cycle, and let it fill with clean water.

6. Stop the action; hand swish and squeeze again.

7. Set the washer to the spin cycle and let it spin out the water. You might need to rinse twice to remove all soap.

8. Remove your quilt, pull it gently and flatten it until you get the correct shape. Use a ruler to make sure it's square. Lay it flat to dry.

About the Author

Pat Durbin is an award-winning quilter and a quilting teacher. She grew up sewing and has enjoyed that talent throughout her life. In recent years she has been making "art" quilts that resemble paintings. She finds this to be filled with challenges and rewards, and she enjoys teaching and sharing her methods. For Pat, sharing is a blessing.

Most of what Pat does begins as a photograph that she uses to make a quilt resembling that photo as closely as possible. She is constantly experimenting with new ways to create art quilts. She has done portraits as well as many landscapes. Her book *Mosaic Picture Quilts: Turn Favorite Photos into Stunning Quilts* (Martingale & Company, 2007) describes the method she devised to make picture quilts using photos as inspiration and tiny squares of fabric in mosaic fashion.

Pat is a minister's wife and lives on the beautiful northern coast of California. She and her husband, Gary, enjoy traveling to view the beautiful land in which we live. Gary takes most of the photographs that Pat uses as inspiration for her quilts. Pat loves experimenting with new methods and adapting old methods to enhance her art. She is active in her church in women's ministries and the music program. She considers her growing family—children, grandchildren, and now great-grandchildren—to be blessings from God.

SEE MORE ONLINE!

- Go to www.patdurbin.com for additional picture outlines, autographed books, and kits and quilts for sale.

- To learn more about *Mosaic Picture Quilts: Turn Favorite Photos into Stunning Quilts*, visit www.martingale-pub.com.

Resources

I always recommend checking at your local stores first. If the item you need isn't available there, try these sources:

DecoArt Paints
SoSoft fabric paints
www.decoart.com

Embroidery Hoops and Art Supplies
Darice Spring Tension embroidery hoops
www.createforless.com

New and Best-Selling Titles from

America's Best-Loved
Quilt Books®

America's Best-Loved Craft & Hobby Books®
America's Best-Loved Knitting Books®

APPLIQUÉ
Appliqué Quilt Revival
Beautiful Blooms
Cutting-Garden Quilts
Dream Landscapes
Easy Appliqué Blocks
Simple Comforts
Sunbonnet Sue and Scottie Too

BABIES AND CHILDREN
Baby's First Quilts
Let's Pretend
Snuggle-and-Learn Quilts for Kids
Sweet and Simple Baby Quilts
Warm Welcome—NEW!

BEGINNER
Color for the Terrified Quilter
Four-Patch Frolic—NEW!
Happy Endings, Revised Edition
Machine Appliqué for the Terrified Quilter
Quilting Your Style—NEW!
Your First Quilt Book (or it should be!)

GENERAL QUILTMAKING
American Jane's Quilts for All Seasons
Bits and Pieces
Bold and Beautiful
Country-Fresh Quilts
Creating Your Perfect Quilting Space
Fat-Quarter Quilting—NEW!
Fig Tree Quilts: Fresh Vintage Sewing
Folk-Art Favorites
Follow-the-Line Quilting Designs
    Volume Three
Gathered from the Garden
The New Handmade
Points of View
Prairie Children and Their Quilts
Quilt Challenge—NEW!
Quilt Revival
A Quilter's Diary
Quilter's Happy Hour

Quilting for Joy
Quilts from Paradise—NEW!
Remembering Adelia
Simple Seasons
Skinny Quilts and Table Runners
Twice Quilted

HOLIDAY AND SEASONAL
Candy Cane Lane—NEW!
Christmas Quilts from Hopscotch
Comfort and Joy
Deck the Halls—NEW!
Holiday Wrappings

HOOKED RUGS, NEEDLE FELTING, AND PUNCHNEEDLE
Miniature Punchneedle Embroidery
Needle Felting with Cotton and Wool
Needle-Felting Magic

PAPER PIECING
A Year of Paper Piecing
Easy Reversible Vests, Revised Edition
Paper-Pieced Mini Quilts
Show Me How to Paper Piece

PIECING
501 Rotary-Cut Quilt Blocks
Favorite Traditional Quilts Made Easy
Loose Change
Mosaic Picture Quilts
New Cuts for New Quilts
On-Point Quilts
Ribbon Star Quilts
Rolling Along

QUICK QUILTS
40 Fabulous Quick-Cut Quilts
Charmed, I'm Sure—NEW!
Instant Bargello
Quilts on the Double
Sew Fun, Sew Colorful Quilts
Supersize 'Em!

SCRAP QUILTS
Nickel Quilts
Save the Scraps
Scrap-Basket Surprises
Simple Strategies for Scrap Quilts

CRAFTS
A to Z of Sewing
Art from the Heart
The Beader's Handbook
Dolly Mama Beads
Embellished Memories
Friendship Bracelets All Grown Up
Making Beautiful Jewelry
Paper It!
Trading Card Treasures

KNITTING & CROCHET
365 Crochet Stitches a Year
365 Knitting Stitches a Year
A to Z of Knitting
All about Crochet—NEW!
All about Knitting
Amigurumi World
Amigurumi Two!—NEW!
Beyond Wool
Cable Confidence
Casual, Elegant Knits
Crocheted Pursenalities
Knitted Finger Puppets
The Knitter's Book of Finishing
    Techniques
Knitting Circles around Socks
*Knitting More Circles around
    Socks—NEW!*
Knits from the North Sea—NEW!
More Sensational Knitted Socks
*New Twists on Twined Knitting—
    NEW!*
Pursenalities
Simple Stitches
Toe-Up Techniques for Hand-
    Knit Socks, Revised Edition
Together or Separate